I Use Help, Too

by Terry Miller Shannon
illustrated by Judy Stead

Shane put his clothes in the drawer.

"Thank you, Shane," Mom said. "You're a big help now."

"I used to help, too!" Shane said.

Mom laughed. "Is that what you'd call it?" she asked. She gave her head a little shake.

"Mom!" Shane said. "I was a big help! I put clothes away on wash day."

"Yes," Mom laughed. "But now you put them away in the right place!"

"I used to help you cook, too," he told her.

Mom said, "I'm not sure I'd call it help!"

"Well," said Shane, "I helped rake leaves."

Mom smiled. "You'd shape them into a pile and jump on them!"

Shane said, "Mom! It's a shame you can't remember! I was always a big help picking up toys."

Mom laughed. She couldn't seem to stop.

Shane tried again. "I liked to help you in the garden, too."

"You are more help in the garden now," Mom said, laughing.

Shane said, "We don't remember things the same!"

Mom hugged him. "Once you were too small to be a big help. But you always helped me smile!"